# CONTENTS

# WHAT CAN ASTROLOGY
## *do for me?*

Astrology is a powerful tool for self-awareness. The idea that we are all connected – that the shifting energies of the Sun, Moon and planets above affect us here on Earth – is an ancient and philosophical belief. Astrology isn't fortune-telling – it can't predict your future and it doesn't deal in absolutes. It simply says that you are part of the universe around you, and by studying the stars, it's possible to learn more about yourself.

Why is this so important? Because the better understanding you have of your own inner make-up – your skills, your talents, your needs and your fears – the more insight you gain into why you act the way you do. And this gives you choices, empowering you to make changes and to build on your strengths. It makes it easier to feel confident and to accept yourself, quirks and all.

There are countless daily horoscopes in newspapers, magazines and online. But this book looks at more than just your star sign, which is only a small part of your personality picture. It helps you to find your Rising sign, which was appearing over the Eastern horizon at the time of your birth, and has a lot to tell you about the way others see you. You can also work out your Moon sign, which reveals the real you deep down inside, giving you the chance to get to grips with your innermost emotions, desires, fears and obsessions.

With a clearer picture of who you are, life becomes less complicated. Instead of trying to live up to others' expectations and being someone you're not, you can work instead on becoming the best version of yourself possible – someone who understands their talents and needs, who is perfectly unique and is happy.

# What is
# ASTROLOGY?

The stars and planets have always inspired a sense of wonder. The ancient peoples of Babylonia, Persia, Egypt, Greece and India were all fascinated by the cycles of the Moon, the rising and setting of the Sun, the position of the constellations and what it all meant. As these civilizations developed, they connected what they saw in the sky with the people and events on Earth, and astrology was born.

In ancient times, astrology was used to help monarchs rule. Kings and emperors would employ astrologers to predict the weather, speak to the gods and help manage the country.

Modern astrology has evolved to help ordinary people like you and me understand ourselves better – how we behave, how we feel about each other and how we can make the best of who we are.

# THE SIGNS OF THE ZODIAC

Today we know that the planets revolve around the Sun, but astrology is based on how we see the solar system from here on Earth. The Zodiac is a group of 12 constellations that, from our viewpoint, seem to rotate around Earth over the course of a year, like a huge wheel. These constellations are named after the animals and objects that our ancestors thought they looked most like – the ram, the lion, the scorpion and so on. Your Sun sign tells you which of the constellations the Sun was moving through on the day you were born. The signs have a natural order that never varies, beginning with Aries. The dates given on the right change slightly from year to year for the same reasons we have a leap year – each of our days is slightly longer than 24 hours. If you were born at the beginning or end of a sign, called 'the cusp', it's worth checking your Sun sign online to be sure.

| ARIES | LIBRA |
|---|---|
| March 21–April 20 | September 23–October 22 |
| TAURUS | SCORPIO |
| April 21–May 21 | October 23–November 21 |
| GEMINI | SAGITTARIUS |
| May 22–June 21 | November 22–December 21 |
| CANCER | CAPRICORN |
| June 22–July 22 | December 22–January 20 |
| LEO | AQUARIUS |
| July 23–August 23 | January 21–February 19 |
| VIRGO | PISCES |
| August 24–September 22 | February 20–March 20 |

# THE FOUR ELEMENTS

*Each Sun sign is associated with one of four elements –
Fire, Earth, Air and Water.*

## FIRE

**Aries, Leo, Sagittarius**
*Fire signs are passionate, dynamic and temperamental.*
**They mix well with:** Fire and Air types

## EARTH

**Taurus, Virgo, Capricorn**
*Earth signs are practical, cautious and reliable.*
**They mix well with:** Water and Earth types

## AIR

**Gemini, Libra, Aquarius**
*Air signs are quick, curious and adventurous.*
**They mix well with:** Air and Fire types

## WATER

**Cancer, Scorpio, Pisces**
*Water signs are sensitive, emotional and kind.*
**They mix well with:** Earth and Water types

# THE PLANETS

Astrology looks at the positions of the stars and planets at the time and place of your birth. The Sun and Moon aren't technically planets, but they're referred to that way by astrologers for ease of use. The Sun is a great place to start – it's the most important object in the solar system. Your Sun sign describes the essence of your identity and says a great deal about your potential – the person you might become.

The position the Moon held in the sky at the time of your birth has a strong influence, too. It describes your emotions – how you feel deep inside. It can give you a better understanding of what you need to feel loved and cared for.

And there's also your Rising sign. This is the sign of the Zodiac that was appearing over the Eastern horizon at the time of your birth. It tells you more about how you interact with the world around you, especially to new situations. It's the filter through which you perceive the world and the impression you give to others on first meeting. Which means it's also how others often see you.

The positions of the other planets – Venus, Mercury, Mars, etc – in your birth chart all have their own effect. But these three taken together – Sun, Moon and Rising sign – will give you a deeper understanding of who you are and what you could become, your strengths and weaknesses, your real self.

# Your SUN sign

# SCORPIO

### October 23–November 21

**SYMBOL**
The Scorpion

**ELEMENT**
Water

**RULING PLANET**
Pluto

**BIRTHSTONE**
Topaz

**COLOUR**
Burgundy

**BODY PART**
Pelvis

**DAY OF THE WEEK**
Friday

**FLOWER**
Geranium

**CHARACTER TRAITS**
Powerful, mysterious, magnetic

**KEY PHRASE**
'I desire'

# YOUR SUN SIGN

When people talk about astrology and ask about your star sign, they're referring to your Sun sign. It tells you which of the 12 constellations of the Zodiac the Sun was moving through on the day you were born. This makes it easy to work out, which is one of the reasons for its popularity. If you'd like to know the Sun sign of a friend or family member, the table on page 7 shows which days the Sun occupies each of the signs over the course of a year.

The Sun is the heart of your chart – it's the essence of who you are and symbolizes the potential of what you can achieve. It's important to remember, though, that it is only a part of the whole picture when it comes to astrology. It's a wonderful starting point, but there are many other layers encasing your core identity, all of which affect the inner you.

## ALL ABOUT YOU

Born with the Sun in Scorpio, you have the potential to be a powerful force for change and to inspire and empower others to be the best they can be. Mysterious and complex, you have an uncanny ability to see right to the heart of things. As a Water sign, your senses are tuned in to others' emotions, so much so people around you don't bother trying to hide anything – they know you'll see straight through them.

Although some Scorpions can have that famous sting in their tail, most of you are pretty chilled out – as long as you're headed to where you want to go. That's because you live life to the fullest: there's no half measures here.

For the friends who come along for the ride, it's a thrilling experience. You love a bit of drama in your life, and things are never dull.

You have a strong competitive streak and are always throwing down the gauntlet to your friends – whether it's a football game or a sing-off. You like to win, and your challenge is to learn to accept defeat graciously.

Fiercely loyal, you expect the devotion you show your friends to be 100 per cent returned. You also have the memory of an elephant – if someone upsets you, there's a tendency to hold onto that hurt. Letting things go isn't your strong suit, but your ability to bounce back after a difficult experience is inspirational.

## Likes

Being in control
Privacy
Scary stories
Looking mysterious
Making decisions
The paranormal

## Dislikes

Asking for help
Failure
Being teased

## HOW TO BRING OUT YOUR BEST

Water is thought to represent emotions and, as a Scorpio, your feelings run deep. You might be puzzled, and maybe even a little jealous, at the ease with which things seem to roll off your friends' backs. But that's the beauty of friendship: we all learn from each other.

When you set your mind to something, nothing will stand in your way. Charming and sincere, you are quietly commanding. If someone says or does something you don't agree with, you're happy to call them out.

At your core, though, you have oodles of kindness and a deep desire to make the world a better place. You're the one to persuade others to think about voluntary work or doing something for their community. And your sensitivity to others' feelings means you're always the one to notice when someone's upset, even if it doesn't show on their face. If they need to talk, you'll be their rock to lean on. Just remember, they can be there for you, too, when you need it. Knowing when to ask for help is a strength, not a weakness.

## Strengths

Loyal
Passionate
Sensitive
Driven
Strong
Resourceful
Motivated

## Weaknesses

Jealous
Lonely
Distrustful

## SECRET FEARS

You are excellent at hiding your fears from everyone around you. They would never know, for example, how scared you are of failure. You like to be firmly in control of every aspect of your life – it gives you a sense of security – and you can spin off into panic when you're not.

By opening up to those people you trust – your friends and family – you'll be able to overcome these feelings far quicker than if you keep everything to yourself. It might be a little scary at first, but the payoff is worth it. When you decide you are ready to let a new friend into your life, you can be secretly worried it won't go the distance. Taking emotional risks will help to build your confidence even more.

. . . . . . . . . . . . . . . . . . . . . . . . . . . . . . . . . . . . . . . . . . . . . . . . . . . . . . . . . . . . . . . . . . . . . . . . . . . . . . . . . . . . . .

## Most likely to . . .

Know what you want

Hold a grudge

Say, 'Guys, I think I might actually be psychic'

Stick up for friends

Think you're right

Push yourself

Tell the truth

Keep a secret

# Your RISING sign

# YOUR RISING SIGN

Your Rising sign, also known as your Ascendant, is the sign that was rising over the Eastern horizon (the place where the Sun rises each day) when you were born. It describes how you see the world and the people around you and how they see you – the first impression that you give and receive, the image you project and the initial reaction you might have to a new situation. A person with Leo Rising, for example, may strike you as warm and engaging, whereas Pisces Rising is more sensitive and possibly shy. Because the Ascendant is determined by the exact time and place you were born, it is the most personal point in your chart. Many astrologers believe this makes it just as important as your Sun sign.

## HOW TO FIND YOUR ASCENDANT

This is where it gets a bit tricky. There's a reason that popular astrology only deals with your Sun sign – your Rising sign can be more difficult to work out. But don't be put off. If you know your Sun sign and your time of birth, you can use the table on the right to give you a good idea. To be totally accurate you do need to take into account factors like time zone and daylight savings, and there are plenty of free online calculators that will do just that.

| YOUR SUN SIGN | YOUR HOUR OF BIRTH | | | | | | | | | | | |
|---|---|---|---|---|---|---|---|---|---|---|---|---|
| | 6:00 AM to 8:00 AM | 8:00 AM to 10:00 AM | 10:00 AM to 12:00 PM | 12:00 PM to 2:00 PM | 2:00 PM to 4:00 PM | 4:00 PM to 6:00 PM | 6:00 PM to 8:00 PM | 8:00 PM to 10:00 PM | 10:00 PM to 12:00 AM | 12:00 AM to 2:00 AM | 2:00 AM to 4:00 AM | 4:00 AM to 6:00 AM |
| ARIES ♈ | ♉ | ♊ | ♋ | ♌ | ♍ | ♎ | ♏ | ♐ | ♑ | ♒ | ♓ | ♈ |
| TAURUS ♉ | ♊ | ♋ | ♌ | ♍ | ♎ | ♏ | ♐ | ♑ | ♒ | ♓ | ♈ | ♉ |
| GEMINI ♊ | ♋ | ♌ | ♍ | ♎ | ♏ | ♐ | ♑ | ♒ | ♓ | ♈ | ♉ | ♊ |
| CANCER ♋ | ♌ | ♍ | ♎ | ♏ | ♐ | ♑ | ♒ | ♓ | ♈ | ♉ | ♊ | ♋ |
| LEO ♌ | ♍ | ♎ | ♏ | ♐ | ♑ | ♒ | ♓ | ♈ | ♉ | ♊ | ♋ | ♌ |
| VIRGO ♍ | ♎ | ♏ | ♐ | ♑ | ♒ | ♓ | ♈ | ♉ | ♊ | ♋ | ♌ | ♍ |
| LIBRA ♎ | ♏ | ♐ | ♑ | ♒ | ♓ | ♈ | ♉ | ♊ | ♋ | ♌ | ♍ | ♎ |
| SCORPIO ♏ | ♐ | ♑ | ♒ | ♓ | ♈ | ♉ | ♊ | ♋ | ♌ | ♍ | ♎ | ♏ |
| SAGITTARIUS ♐ | ♑ | ♒ | ♓ | ♈ | ♉ | ♊ | ♋ | ♌ | ♍ | ♎ | ♏ | ♐ |
| CAPRICORN ♑ | ♒ | ♓ | ♈ | ♉ | ♊ | ♋ | ♌ | ♍ | ♎ | ♏ | ♐ | ♑ |
| AQUARIUS ♒ | ♓ | ♈ | ♉ | ♊ | ♋ | ♌ | ♍ | ♎ | ♏ | ♐ | ♑ | ♒ |
| PISCES ♓ | ♈ | ♉ | ♊ | ♋ | ♌ | ♍ | ♎ | ♏ | ♐ | ♑ | ♒ | ♓ |

# WHAT YOUR RISING SIGN SAYS ABOUT YOU

*Once you have figured out your Ascendant, you are ready to discover more about how you see the world, and how it sees you.*

### ARIES RISING

Aries is as forthright as you are reticent, so this combination brings balance. You're highly energetic and can come across as daring and impulsive, but people struggle to keep up with you, so it might be a good idea to practise patience. Friends and acquaintances open up to you easily, which satisfies your Scorpio penchant for intrigue. You have a tendency to brood over your intense feelings. At these times, mindfulness can help stop you from getting bogged down in your thoughts.

### TAURUS RISING

You truly enjoy the finer things in life. Designer clothes, expensive restaurants and amazing trips to faraway lands are all high on your agenda. Luckily, Taurus delivers the determination to work hard enough to fund your dream lifestyle. However, it's important to remember that these things won't build the foundation for a happy life – it's wise to invest in your friendships, too. You come across as easy-going, but you might also have a stubborn streak, which close friends soon learn to handle.

### GEMINI RISING

Gemini introduces a strong desire for independence into the Scorpio mix. You can often scatter your energy in too many directions at once, which leaves you jumping all over the place like a grasshopper. While this comes from good intentions – you want to grab life by the tail – you might benefit from consciously considering what your priorities are. While you're a sociable creature, if the conversation gets too personal for your liking, you tend to fall silent, which can confuse your friends.

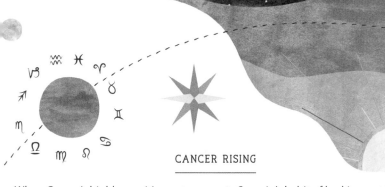

### CANCER RISING

When Cancer's highly sensitive nature meets Scorpio's habit of looking out for potential problems, you can become a little insecure. You might also like to keep your emotions under wraps. Learning to confide in close friends and talk things through can be a great help. After all, wouldn't you do the same for them? Your hands-on attitude, matched with Cancer's love of nature, means you're likely to be a nurturer who delights in watching the seeds you plant grow and blossom.

### LEO RISING

Leo's renowned pride can sometimes accentuate Scorpio's reserved side. You like to feel secure and one step ahead of everyone else, but it's good to keep in mind that a lighter, less cautious approach to life's many ups and downs can help generate more positive outcomes or better ways of dealing with unexpected obstacles. You often amaze people with your competence and courage, and you have the patience and persistence to achieve success in whatever you put your mind to.

### VIRGO RISING

The Virgo drive to understand the world, combined with Scorpio's intuition and sensitivity, makes this a powerful partnership. There's not much that gets past you, and you have an extraordinary talent for figuring out what makes people tick. This insight makes you a fabulous problem-solver who seems to come up with clever solutions almost effortlessly. Friends seek you out for your emotionally intelligent advice. You rarely get a situation wrong, so you'll quickly become the agony aunt or uncle in your circle. Happily, your friends are more than willing to return the favour.

### LIBRA RISING

Libra's ability to assess things lends itself well to Scorpio's talent for getting people to open up. You have a wonderful gift for putting yourself in the other person's shoes, so it's no surprise when a friend in need comes knocking on your door. Scorpios can crave time to themselves, but with Libra as your Rising sign, that's not necessarily the case. You're happiest when surrounded by those you love, sharing stories and secrets, and you have a strong inner confidence that makes you unflappable.

### SCORPIO RISING

With double Scorpio, you can be highly self-motivated and determined to do your absolute best in everything you take on. However, this strong work ethic can be a one-way ticket to emotional exhaustion, so sometimes it's okay to aim for good enough rather than perfection. Your skill in getting to know absolutely everything about friends means you're the keeper of secrets. Your feelings run deep, so try not to blow small disagreements out of proportion.

### SAGITTARIUS RISING

With this combination, wherever you go, people tend to follow. The joy for life that Sagittarius brings, mixed with Scorpio's edginess, means you're often surrounded by an excited entourage, eager to have some of that hypnotic energy rub off on them. You have a relentless determination and the forensic skills necessary to get to the heart of a problem. You might feel the desire to put your friends to the test to see how much they care about you, but have confidence in the fact that they're the real deal.

### CAPRICORN RISING

As the wise sea-goat of the Zodiac, Capricorn tempers Scorpio's dislike of the daily routine, helping you to see projects through to the end. You have a forward-thinking mentality, and this draws like-minded people into your orbit. You're also a natural team player. In your friendship circle, you're known as the quiet one. Rather than grabbing the spotlight, you prefer to take a backseat, discovering and learning by listening intently.

### AQUARIUS RISING

The Aquarian knack for identifying future problems magnifies Scorpio's deeply inquisitive nature. You can often be on high alert, which makes you a natural at handling fraught situations, and you generally keep a level head where others might lose their cool. However, learning to switch off is advisable. Perhaps add breathing techniques and relaxing yoga to your self-care kit bag – you'll notice the positive effect they have on your friendships. When you switch to the lighter, less serious side of your personality, you'll find friends clamour for your company.

### PISCES RISING

Peacemaker Pisces softens the sting-in-the-tail quality of Scorpio. You're not a fan of confrontation and are usually highly skilled in defusing potentially explosive situations. So, if two friends are getting on each other's nerves, you have the ability to quickly calm the situation before it develops into a full-blown argument. You tend to have a compassionate nature and take pleasure in caring for other people and animals. Remember to show the same compassion towards yourself.

# Your MOON sign

# YOUR MOON SIGN

The Moon rules your emotions and your inner moods, telling you what you need to feel safe, comfortable and loved. Knowing your Moon sign should give you a more complete picture of your unique self, helping you to express needs you might be struggling to understand. Suppose your Sun sign is Aries but being first has never been important to you – a Moon in Virgo may be telling you to hang back and fade into the background. Or you might have the Sun in home-loving Cancer but feel an urge to get out there and see the world. Perhaps that's because your Moon is in freedom-loving Sagittarius

## HOW TO FIND YOUR MOON SIGN

Just like your Rising sign, finding your Moon sign is more complicated than finding your Sun sign. That's because the Moon seems to move so quickly, taking just about a month to pass through all of the constellations. Thankfully, the tables on the right and on the next page make finding it a simple process.

First, find your year of birth. Then locate your birth month at the top of the table. Find your date of birth in the column below it, and this will give you your Moon sign. If your date of birth isn't listed, the one before it is your Moon sign.

*For example, suppose your date of birth is 4 March, 1995. The date before this is 2 March, for which the Moon sign is Aries. This would mean your Moon sign is Aries.*

| JAN | FEB | MAR | APR | MAY | JUN | JUL | AUG | SEP | OCT | NOV | DEC |
|-----|-----|-----|-----|-----|-----|-----|-----|-----|-----|-----|-----|
| **BORN IN THE YEAR 1995** | | | | | | | | | | | |
| 2 Aqu | 1 Pis | 2 Ari | 1 Tau | 1 Gem | 2 Leo | 2 Vir | 3 Sco | 1 Sag | 2 Aqu | 1 Pis | 3 Tau |
| 4 Pis | 3 Ari | 5 Tau | 3 Gem | 3 Can | 5 Vir | 4 Lib | 5 Sag | 3 Cap | 5 Pis | 3 Ari | 5 Gem |
| 7 Ari | 5 Tau | 7 Gem | 6 Can | 6 Leo | 7 Lib | 6 Sco | 7 Cap | 5 Aqu | 7 Ari | 5 Tau | 8 Can |
| 9 Tau | 8 Gem | 10 Can | 9 Leo | 8 Vir | 9 Sco | 8 Sag | 9 Aqu | 7 Pis | 9 Tau | 8 Gem | 10 Leo |
| 12 Gem | 10 Can | 12 Leo | 11 Vir | 10 Lib | 11 Sag | 10 Cap | 11 Pis | 9 Ari | 12 Gem | 10 Can | 13 Vir |
| 14 Can | 13 Leo | 14 Vir | 13 Lib | 13 Sco | 13 Cap | 12 Aqu | 13 Ari | 12 Tau | 14 Can | 13 Leo | 15 Lib |
| 16 Leo | 15 Vir | 17 Lib | 15 Sco | 15 Sag | 15 Aqu | 14 Pis | 15 Tau | 14 Gem | 17 Leo | 15 Vir | 17 Sco |
| 19 Vir | 17 Lib | 19 Sco | 17 Sag | 17 Cap | 17 Pis | 17 Ari | 18 Gem | 17 Can | 19 Vir | 18 Lib | 19 Sag |
| 21 Lib | 19 Sco | 21 Sag | 19 Cap | 19 Aqu | 19 Ari | 19 Tau | 20 Can | 19 Leo | 21 Lib | 20 Sco | 21 Cap |
| 23 Sco | 22 Sag | 23 Cap | 21 Aqu | 21 Pis | 22 Tau | 22 Gem | 23 Leo | 22 Vir | 23 Sco | 22 Sag | 23 Aqu |
| 25 Sag | 24 Cap | 25 Aqu | 24 Pis | 23 Ari | 24 Gem | 24 Can | 25 Vir | 24 Lib | 26 Sag | 24 Cap | 25 Pis |
| 27 Cap | 26 Aqu | 27 Pis | 26 Ari | 26 Tau | 27 Can | 27 Leo | 28 Lib | 26 Sco | 28 Cap | 26 Aqu | 28 Ari |
| 30 Aqu | 28 Pis | 30 Ari | 28 Tau | 28 Gem | 29 Leo | 29 Vir | 30 Sco | 28 Sag | 30 Aqu | 28 Pis | 30 Tau |
| | | | | 31 Can | | 31 Lib | | 30 Cap | | 30 Ari | |
| **BORN IN THE YEAR 1996** | | | | | | | | | | | |
| 1 Gem | 3 Leo | 1 Leo | 2 Lib | 2 Sco | 2 Cap | 2 Aqu | 2 Ari | 1 Tau | 3 Can | 2 Leo | 2 Vir |
| 4 Can | 5 Vir | 3 Vir | 4 Sco | 4 Sag | 4 Aqu | 4 Pis | 4 Tau | 3 Gem | 5 Leo | 4 Vir | 4 Lib |
| 6 Leo | 8 Lib | 6 Lib | 7 Sag | 6 Cap | 6 Pis | 6 Ari | 7 Gem | 6 Can | 8 Vir | 7 Lib | 6 Sco |
| 9 Vir | 10 Sco | 8 Sco | 9 Cap | 8 Aqu | 9 Ari | 8 Tau | 9 Can | 8 Leo | 10 Lib | 9 Sco | 9 Sag |
| 11 Lib | 12 Sag | 10 Sag | 11 Aqu | 10 Pis | 11 Tau | 11 Gem | 12 Leo | 11 Vir | 13 Sco | 11 Sag | 11 Cap |
| 14 Sco | 14 Cap | 13 Cap | 13 Pis | 12 Ari | 13 Gem | 13 Can | 14 Vir | 13 Lib | 15 Sag | 13 Cap | 13 Aqu |
| 16 Sag | 16 Aqu | 15 Aqu | 15 Ari | 15 Tau | 16 Can | 16 Leo | 17 Lib | 15 Sco | 17 Cap | 16 Aqu | 15 Pis |
| 18 Cap | 18 Pis | 17 Pis | 17 Tau | 17 Gem | 18 Leo | 18 Vir | 19 Sco | 18 Sag | 19 Aqu | 18 Pis | 17 Ari |
| 20 Aqu | 20 Ari | 19 Ari | 20 Gem | 19 Can | 21 Vir | 21 Lib | 21 Sag | 20 Cap | 21 Pis | 20 Ari | 19 Tau |
| 22 Pis | 23 Tau | 21 Tau | 22 Can | 22 Leo | 23 Lib | 23 Sco | 24 Cap | 22 Aqu | 23 Ari | 22 Tau | 22 Gem |
| 24 Ari | 25 Gem | 23 Gem | 25 Leo | 25 Vir | 26 Sco | 25 Sag | 26 Aqu | 24 Pis | 26 Tau | 24 Gem | 24 Can |
| 26 Tau | 27 Can | 26 Can | 27 Vir | 27 Lib | 28 Sag | 27 Cap | 28 Pis | 26 Ari | 28 Gem | 27 Can | 26 Leo |
| 29 Gem | | 28 Leo | 30 Lib | 29 Sco | 30 Cap | 29 Aqu | 30 Ari | 28 Tau | 30 Can | 29 Leo | 29 Vir |
| 31 Can | | 31 Vir | | 31 Sag | | 31 Pis | | 30 Gem | | | 31 Lib |
| **BORN IN THE YEAR 1997** | | | | | | | | | | | |
| 3 Sco | 1 Sag | 1 Sag | 1 Aqu | 1 Pis | 1 Tau | 1 Gem | 2 Leo | 3 Lib | 3 Sco | 1 Sag | 1 Cap |
| 5 Sag | 4 Cap | 3 Cap | 4 Pis | 3 Ari | 4 Gem | 3 Can | 4 Vir | 6 Sco | 5 Sag | 4 Cap | 3 Aqu |
| 7 Cap | 6 Aqu | 5 Aqu | 6 Ari | 5 Tau | 6 Can | 5 Leo | 7 Lib | 8 Sag | 8 Cap | 6 Aqu | 5 Pis |
| 9 Aqu | 8 Pis | 7 Pis | 8 Tau | 7 Gem | 8 Leo | 8 Vir | 9 Sco | 10 Cap | 10 Aqu | 8 Pis | 8 Ari |
| 11 Pis | 10 Ari | 9 Ari | 10 Gem | 9 Can | 11 Vir | 10 Lib | 12 Sag | 12 Aqu | 12 Pis | 10 Ari | 10 Tau |
| 13 Ari | 12 Tau | 11 Tau | 12 Can | 12 Leo | 13 Lib | 13 Sco | 14 Cap | 15 Pis | 14 Ari | 12 Tau | 12 Gem |
| 15 Tau | 14 Gem | 13 Gem | 14 Leo | 14 Vir | 16 Sco | 15 Sag | 16 Aqu | 17 Ari | 16 Tau | 14 Gem | 14 Can |
| 18 Gem | 16 Can | 16 Can | 17 Vir | 17 Lib | 18 Sag | 18 Cap | 18 Pis | 19 Tau | 18 Gem | 17 Can | 16 Leo |
| 20 Can | 19 Leo | 18 Leo | 19 Lib | 19 Sco | 20 Cap | 20 Aqu | 20 Ari | 21 Gem | 20 Can | 19 Leo | 19 Vir |
| 23 Leo | 21 Vir | 21 Vir | 22 Sco | 22 Sag | 22 Aqu | 22 Pis | 22 Tau | 23 Can | 23 Leo | 21 Vir | 21 Lib |
| 25 Vir | 24 Lib | 23 Lib | 24 Sag | 24 Cap | 24 Pis | 24 Ari | 24 Gem | 25 Leo | 25 Vir | 24 Lib | 24 Sco |
| 28 Lib | 26 Sco | 26 Sco | 27 Cap | 26 Aqu | 26 Ari | 26 Tau | 27 Can | 28 Vir | 28 Lib | 26 Sco | 26 Sag |
| 30 Sco | | 28 Sag | 29 Aqu | 28 Pis | 29 Tau | 28 Gem | 29 Leo | 30 Lib | 30 Sco | 29 Sag | 28 Cap |
| | | 30 Cap | | 30 Ari | | 30 Can | 31 Vir | | | | 31 Aqu |
| **BORN IN THE YEAR 1998** | | | | | | | | | | | |
| 2 Pis | 2 Tau | 2 Tau | 2 Can | 2 Leo | 3 Lib | 3 Sco | 2 Sag | 3 Aqu | 2 Pis | 1 Ari | 2 Gem |
| 4 Ari | 4 Gem | 4 Gem | 4 Leo | 4 Vir | 5 Sco | 5 Sag | 4 Cap | 5 Pis | 4 Ari | 3 Tau | 4 Can |
| 6 Tau | 7 Can | 6 Can | 7 Vir | 7 Lib | 8 Sag | 8 Cap | 6 Aqu | 7 Ari | 6 Tau | 5 Gem | 6 Leo |
| 8 Gem | 9 Leo | 8 Leo | 9 Lib | 9 Sco | 10 Cap | 10 Aqu | 8 Pis | 9 Tau | 8 Gem | 7 Can | 9 Vir |
| 10 Can | 11 Vir | 11 Vir | 12 Sco | 12 Sag | 13 Aqu | 12 Pis | 11 Ari | 11 Gem | 10 Can | 9 Leo | 11 Lib |
| 13 Leo | 14 Lib | 13 Lib | 14 Sag | 14 Cap | 15 Pis | 14 Ari | 13 Tau | 13 Can | 13 Leo | 11 Vir | 14 Sco |
| 15 Vir | 16 Sco | 16 Sco | 17 Cap | 16 Aqu | 17 Ari | 16 Tau | 15 Gem | 15 Leo | 15 Vir | 14 Lib | 16 Sag |
| 18 Lib | 19 Sag | 18 Sag | 19 Aqu | 19 Pis | 19 Tau | 18 Gem | 17 Can | 18 Vir | 17 Lib | 16 Sco | 19 Cap |
| 20 Sco | 21 Cap | 20 Cap | 21 Pis | 21 Ari | 21 Gem | 21 Can | 19 Leo | 20 Lib | 20 Sco | 19 Sag | 21 Aqu |
| 23 Sag | 23 Aqu | 23 Aqu | 23 Ari | 23 Tau | 23 Can | 23 Leo | 21 Vir | 23 Sco | 23 Sag | 21 Cap | 23 Pis |
| 25 Cap | 25 Pis | 25 Pis | 25 Tau | 25 Gem | 25 Leo | 25 Vir | 24 Lib | 25 Sag | 25 Cap | 24 Aqu | 25 Ari |
| 27 Aqu | 27 Ari | 27 Ari | 27 Gem | 27 Can | 28 Vir | 28 Lib | 26 Sco | 28 Cap | 27 Aqu | 26 Pis | 28 Tau |
| 29 Pis | | 29 Tau | 29 Can | 29 Leo | 30 Lib | 30 Sco | 29 Sag | 30 Aqu | 30 Pis | 28 Ari | 30 Gem |
| 31 Ari | | 31 Gem | | 31 Vir | | | 31 Cap | | | 30 Tau | |

## BORN IN THE YEAR 1999

| JAN | FEB | MAR | APR | MAY | JUN | JUL | AUG | SEP | OCT | NOV | DEC |
|---|---|---|---|---|---|---|---|---|---|---|---|
| 1 Can | 1 Vir | 1 Vir | 2 Sco | 2 Sag | 3 Aqu | 2 Pis | 1 Ari | 2 Gem | 1 Can | 1 Vir | 1 Lib |
| 3 Leo | 4 Lib | 3 Lib | 4 Sag | 4 Cap | 5 Pis | 5 Ari | 3 Tau | 4 Can | 3 Leo | 4 Lib | 3 Sco |
| 5 Vir | 6 Sco | 6 Sco | 7 Cap | 7 Aqu | 8 Ari | 7 Tau | 5 Gem | 6 Leo | 5 Vir | 6 Sco | 6 Sag |
| 7 Lib | 9 Sag | 8 Sag | 9 Aqu | 9 Pis | 10 Tau | 9 Gem | 7 Can | 8 Vir | 8 Lib | 9 Sag | 8 Cap |
| 10 Sco | 11 Cap | 11 Cap | 12 Pis | 11 Ari | 12 Gem | 11 Can | 9 Leo | 10 Lib | 10 Sco | 11 Cap | 11 Aqu |
| 12 Sag | 14 Aqu | 13 Aqu | 14 Ari | 14 Tau | 14 Can | 13 Leo | 12 Vir | 13 Sco | 12 Sag | 14 Aqu | 13 Pis |
| 15 Cap | 16 Pis | 15 Pis | 16 Tau | 15 Gem | 16 Leo | 15 Vir | 14 Lib | 15 Sag | 15 Cap | 16 Pis | 16 Ari |
| 17 Aqu | 18 Ari | 17 Ari | 18 Gem | 17 Can | 18 Vir | 17 Lib | 16 Sco | 18 Cap | 17 Aqu | 18 Ari | 18 Tau |
| 19 Pis | 20 Tau | 19 Tau | 20 Can | 19 Leo | 20 Lib | 20 Sco | 19 Sag | 20 Aqu | 20 Pis | 21 Tau | 20 Gem |
| 22 Ari | 22 Gem | 21 Gem | 22 Leo | 21 Vir | 23 Sco | 22 Sag | 21 Cap | 22 Pis | 22 Ari | 23 Gem | 22 Can |
| 24 Tau | 24 Can | 23 Can | 24 Vir | 24 Lib | 25 Sag | 25 Cap | 24 Aqu | 25 Ari | 24 Tau | 25 Can | 24 Leo |
| 26 Gem | 26 Leo | 26 Leo | 27 Lib | 26 Sco | 28 Cap | 27 Aqu | 26 Pis | 27 Tau | 26 Gem | 27 Leo | 26 Vir |
| 28 Can | | 28 Vir | 29 Sco | 29 Sag | 30 Aqu | 30 Pis | 28 Ari | 29 Gem | 28 Can | 29 Vir | 28 Lib |
| 30 Leo | | 30 Lib | | 31 Cap | | | 30 Tau | | 30 Leo | | 31 Sco |

## BORN IN THE YEAR 2000

| JAN | FEB | MAR | APR | MAY | JUN | JUL | AUG | SEP | OCT | NOV | DEC |
|---|---|---|---|---|---|---|---|---|---|---|---|
| 3 Sag | 1 Cap | 2 Aqu | 1 Pis | 3 Tau | 1 Gem | 2 Leo | 1 Vir | 2 Sco | 1 Sag | 3 Aqu | 2 Pis |
| 5 Cap | 4 Aqu | 4 Pis | 3 Ari | 5 Gem | 3 Can | 4 Vir | 3 Lib | 4 Sag | 4 Cap | 5 Pis | 5 Ari |
| 7 Aqu | 6 Pis | 7 Ari | 5 Tau | 7 Can | 5 Leo | 7 Lib | 5 Sco | 6 Cap | 6 Aqu | 8 Ari | 7 Tau |
| 10 Pis | 8 Ari | 9 Tau | 7 Gem | 9 Leo | 7 Vir | 9 Sco | 8 Sag | 9 Aqu | 9 Pis | 10 Tau | 9 Gem |
| 12 Ari | 11 Tau | 11 Gem | 9 Can | 11 Vir | 9 Lib | 11 Sag | 10 Cap | 11 Pis | 11 Ari | 12 Gem | 11 Can |
| 14 Tau | 13 Gem | 13 Can | 11 Leo | 13 Lib | 12 Sco | 14 Cap | 13 Aqu | 14 Ari | 13 Tau | 14 Can | 13 Leo |
| 16 Gem | 15 Can | 15 Leo | 14 Vir | 15 Sco | 14 Sag | 16 Aqu | 15 Pis | 16 Tau | 16 Gem | 16 Leo | 15 Vir |
| 18 Can | 17 Leo | 17 Vir | 16 Lib | 18 Sag | 17 Cap | 19 Pis | 18 Ari | 18 Gem | 18 Can | 18 Vir | 18 Lib |
| 20 Leo | 19 Vir | 20 Lib | 18 Sco | 20 Cap | 19 Aqu | 21 Ari | 20 Tau | 20 Can | 20 Leo | 20 Lib | 20 Sco |
| 23 Vir | 21 Lib | 22 Sco | 20 Sag | 23 Aqu | 22 Pis | 24 Tau | 22 Gem | 23 Leo | 22 Vir | 23 Sco | 22 Sag |
| 25 Lib | 23 Sco | 24 Sag | 23 Cap | 25 Pis | 24 Ari | 26 Gem | 24 Can | 25 Vir | 24 Lib | 25 Sag | 25 Cap |
| 27 Sco | 26 Sag | 27 Cap | 26 Aqu | 28 Ari | 26 Tau | 28 Can | 26 Leo | 27 Lib | 26 Sco | 27 Cap | 27 Aqu |
| 29 Sag | 28 Cap | 29 Aqu | 28 Pis | 30 Tau | 28 Gem | 30 Leo | 28 Vir | 29 Sco | 29 Sag | 30 Aqu | 30 Pis |
| | | | 30 Ari | | 30 Can | | 30 Lib | | 31 Cap | | |

## BORN IN THE YEAR 2001

| JAN | FEB | MAR | APR | MAY | JUN | JUL | AUG | SEP | OCT | NOV | DEC |
|---|---|---|---|---|---|---|---|---|---|---|---|
| 1 Ari | 2 Gem | 1 Gem | 2 Leo | 1 Vir | 2 Sco | 1 Sag | 3 Agu | 1 Pis | 1 Ari | 2 Gem | 2 Can |
| 4 Tau | 4 Can | 4 Can | 4 Vir | 3 Lib | 4 Sag | 4 Cap | 5 Pis | 4 Ari | 4 Tau | 4 Can | 4 Leo |
| 6 Gem | 6 Leo | 6 Leo | 6 Lib | 5 Sco | 7 Cap | 6 Aqu | 8 Ari | 6 Tau | 6 Gem | 7 Leo | 6 Vir |
| 8 Can | 8 Vir | 8 Vir | 8 Sco | 8 Sag | 9 Aqu | 9 Pis | 10 Tau | 9 Gem | 8 Can | 9 Vir | 8 Lib |
| 10 Leo | 10 Lib | 10 Lib | 10 Sag | 10 Cap | 11 Pis | 11 Ari | 12 Gem | 11 Can | 10 Leo | 11 Lib | 10 Sco |
| 12 Vir | 12 Sco | 12 Sco | 13 Cap | 13 Aqu | 14 Ari | 14 Tau | 15 Can | 13 Leo | 13 Vir | 13 Sco | 12 Sag |
| 14 Lib | 15 Sag | 14 Sag | 15 Aqu | 15 Pis | 16 Tau | 16 Gem | 17 Leo | 15 Vir | 15 Lib | 15 Sag | 15 Cap |
| 16 Sco | 17 Cap | 16 Cap | 18 Pis | 18 Ari | 19 Gem | 18 Can | 19 Vir | 17 Lib | 17 Sco | 17 Cap | 17 Aqu |
| 18 Sag | 20 Aqu | 18 Pis | 20 Ari | 20 Tau | 21 Can | 20 Leo | 21 Lib | 19 Sco | 19 Sag | 20 Aqu | 20 Pis |
| 21 Cap | 22 Pis | 22 Pis | 23 Tau | 22 Gem | 23 Leo | 22 Vir | 23 Sco | 21 Sag | 21 Cap | 22 Pis | 22 Ari |
| 23 Aqu | 25 Ari | 24 Ari | 25 Gem | 24 Can | 25 Vir | 24 Lib | 25 Sag | 24 Cap | 23 Aqu | 25 Ari | 25 Tau |
| 26 Pis | 27 Tau | 26 Tau | 27 Can | 27 Leo | 27 Lib | 26 Sco | 27 Cap | 26 Aqu | 26 Pis | 27 Tau | 27 Gem |
| 28 Ari | | 29 Gem | 29 Leo | 29 Vir | 29 Sco | 29 Sag | 30 Aqu | 29 Pis | 28 Ari | 30 Gem | 29 Can |
| 31 Tau | | 31 Can | | 31 Lib | | 31 Cap | | | 31 Tau | | 31 Leo |

## BORN IN THE YEAR 2002

| JAN | FEB | MAR | APR | MAY | JUN | JUL | AUG | SEP | OCT | NOV | DEC |
|---|---|---|---|---|---|---|---|---|---|---|---|
| 2 Vir | 1 Lib | 2 Sco | 1 Sag | 2 Aqu | 1 Pis | 1 Ari | 2 Gem | 1 Can | 1 Leo | 1 Lib | 1 Sco |
| 4 Lib | 3 Sco | 4 Sag | 3 Cap | 5 Pis | 4 Ari | 4 Tau | 5 Can | 3 Leo | 3 Vir | 3 Sco | 3 Sag |
| 6 Sco | 5 Sag | 6 Cap | 5 Aqu | 7 Ari | 6 Tau | 6 Gem | 7 Leo | 5 Vir | 5 Lib | 5 Sag | 5 Cap |
| 9 Sag | 7 Cap | 9 Aqu | 8 Pis | 10 Tau | 9 Gem | 8 Can | 9 Vir | 7 Lib | 7 Sco | 7 Cap | 7 Aqu |
| 11 Cap | 10 Aqu | 11 Pis | 10 Ari | 12 Gem | 11 Can | 11 Leo | 11 Lib | 9 Sco | 9 Sag | 9 Aqu | 9 Pis |
| 13 Aqu | 12 Pis | 14 Ari | 13 Tau | 14 Can | 13 Leo | 13 Vir | 13 Sco | 12 Sag | 12 Cap | 12 Pis | 11 Ari |
| 16 Pis | 15 Ari | 16 Tau | 15 Gem | 17 Leo | 15 Vir | 15 Lib | 15 Sag | 14 Cap | 13 Aqu | 15 Ari | 14 Tau |
| 18 Ari | 17 Tau | 19 Gem | 18 Can | 19 Vir | 18 Lib | 17 Sco | 18 Cap | 16 Aqu | 16 Pis | 17 Tau | 17 Gem |
| 21 Tau | 20 Gem | 21 Can | 20 Leo | 21 Lib | 20 Sco | 19 Sag | 20 Aqu | 19 Pis | 18 Ari | 20 Gem | 19 Can |
| 23 Gem | 22 Can | 24 Leo | 22 Vir | 23 Sco | 22 Sag | 21 Cap | 22 Pis | 21 Ari | 21 Tau | 22 Can | 22 Leo |
| 26 Can | 24 Leo | 26 Vir | 24 Lib | 25 Sag | 24 Cap | 24 Aqu | 25 Ari | 24 Tau | 23 Gem | 24 Leo | 24 Vir |
| 28 Leo | 26 Vir | 28 Lib | 26 Sco | 28 Cap | 26 Aqu | 26 Pis | 27 Tau | 26 Gem | 26 Can | 27 Vir | 26 Sco |
| 30 Vir | 28 Lib | 30 Sco | 28 Sag | 30 Aqu | 29 Pis | 28 Ari | 30 Gem | 29 Can | 28 Leo | 29 Lib | 28 Sco |
| | | | 30 Cap | | | 31 Tau | | | 30 Vir | | 30 Sag |

| JAN | FEB | MAR | APR | MAY | JUN | JUL | AUG | SEP | OCT | NOV | DEC |
|---|---|---|---|---|---|---|---|---|---|---|---|
| 1 Cap | 2 Pis | 1 Pis | 3 Tau | 2 Gem | 1 Can | 1 Leo | 2 Lib | 2 Sag | 1 Cap | 2 Pis | 2 Ari |
| 3 Aqu | 5 Ari | 4 Ari | 5 Gem | 5 Can | 4 Leo | 3 Vir | 4 Sco | 4 Cap | 4 Aqu | 5 Ari | 4 Tau |
| 6 Pis | 7 Tau | 6 Tau | 8 Can | 7 Leo | 6 Vir | 5 Lib | 6 Sag | 6 Aqu | 6 Pis | 7 Tau | 7 Gem |
| 8 Ari | 10 Gem | 9 Gem | 10 Leo | 10 Vir | 8 Lib | 7 Sco | 8 Cap | 9 Pis | 8 Ari | 10 Gem | 9 Can |
| 11 Tau | 12 Can | 11 Can | 12 Vir | 12 Lib | 10 Sco | 10 Sag | 10 Aqu | 11 Ari | 11 Tau | 12 Can | 12 Leo |
| 13 Gem | 14 Leo | 14 Leo | 14 Lib | 14 Sco | 12 Sag | 12 Cap | 12 Pis | 13 Tau | 13 Gem | 15 Leo | 14 Vir |
| 16 Can | 16 Vir | 16 Vir | 16 Sco | 16 Sag | 14 Cap | 14 Aqu | 15 Ari | 16 Gem | 16 Can | 17 Vir | 16 Lib |
| 18 Leo | 18 Lib | 18 Lib | 18 Sag | 18 Cap | 16 Aqu | 16 Pis | 17 Tau | 18 Can | 18 Leo | 19 Lib | 19 Sco |
| 20 Vir | 21 Sco | 20 Sco | 20 Cap | 20 Aqu | 19 Pis | 18 Ari | 20 Gem | 21 Leo | 21 Vir | 21 Sco | 21 Sag |
| 22 Lib | 23 Sag | 22 Sag | 23 Aqu | 22 Pis | 21 Ari | 21 Tau | 22 Can | 23 Vir | 23 Lib | 23 Sag | 23 Cap |
| 24 Sco | 25 Cap | 24 Cap | 25 Pis | 25 Ari | 23 Tau | 23 Gem | 24 Leo | 25 Lib | 25 Sco | 25 Cap | 25 Aqu |
| 26 Sag | 27 Aqu | 26 Aqu | 27 Ari | 27 Tau | 26 Gem | 26 Can | 27 Vir | 27 Sco | 27 Sag | 27 Aqu | 27 Pis |
| 29 Cap | | 29 Pis | 30 Tau | 30 Gem | 28 Can | 28 Leo | 29 Lib | 29 Sag | 29 Cap | 29 Pis | 29 Ari |
| 31 Aqu | | 31 Ari | | | | 30 Vir | 31 Sco | | 31 Aqu | | |

| JAN | FEB | MAR | APR | MAY | JUN | JUL | AUG | SEP | OCT | NOV | DEC |
|---|---|---|---|---|---|---|---|---|---|---|---|
| 1 Tau | 2 Can | 3 Leo | 1 Vir | 1 Lib | 2 Sag | 1 Cap | 1 Pis | 2 Tau | 2 Gem | 1 Can | 1 Leo |
| 3 Gem | 4 Leo | 5 Vir | 4 Lib | 3 Sco | 4 Cap | 3 Aqu | 4 Ari | 5 Gem | 5 Can | 3 Leo | 3 Vir |
| 6 Can | 7 Vir | 7 Lib | 6 Sco | 5 Sag | 6 Aqu | 5 Pis | 6 Tau | 7 Can | 7 Leo | 6 Vir | 6 Lib |
| 8 Leo | 9 Lib | 9 Sco | 8 Sag | 7 Cap | 8 Pis | 7 Ari | 8 Gem | 10 Leo | 10 Vir | 8 Lib | 8 Sco |
| 10 Vir | 11 Sco | 12 Sag | 10 Cap | 9 Aqu | 10 Ari | 10 Tau | 11 Can | 12 Vir | 12 Lib | 10 Sco | 10 Sag |
| 13 Lib | 13 Sag | 14 Cap | 12 Aqu | 11 Pis | 12 Tau | 12 Gem | 13 Leo | 14 Lib | 14 Sco | 13 Sag | 12 Cap |
| 15 Sco | 15 Cap | 16 Aqu | 14 Pis | 14 Ari | 15 Gem | 15 Can | 16 Vir | 17 Sco | 16 Sag | 15 Cap | 14 Aqu |
| 17 Sag | 17 Aqu | 18 Pis | 16 Ari | 16 Tau | 17 Can | 17 Leo | 18 Lib | 19 Sag | 18 Cap | 17 Aqu | 16 Pis |
| 19 Cap | 20 Pis | 20 Ari | 19 Tau | 19 Gem | 20 Leo | 20 Vir | 20 Sco | 21 Cap | 20 Aqu | 19 Pis | 18 Ari |
| 21 Aqu | 22 Ari | 23 Tau | 21 Gem | 21 Can | 22 Vir | 22 Lib | 23 Sag | 23 Aqu | 23 Pis | 21 Ari | 21 Tau |
| 23 Pis | 24 Tau | 25 Gem | 24 Can | 24 Leo | 24 Lib | 24 Sco | 25 Cap | 25 Pis | 25 Ari | 23 Tau | 23 Gem |
| 25 Ari | 27 Gem | 28 Can | 26 Leo | 26 Vir | 27 Sco | 26 Sag | 27 Aqu | 27 Ari | 27 Tau | 26 Gem | 25 Can |
| 28 Tau | 29 Can | 30 Leo | 29 Vir | 28 Lib | 29 Sag | 28 Cap | 29 Pis | 30 Tau | 29 Gem | 28 Can | 28 Leo |
| 30 Gem | | | | 31 Sco | | 30 Aqu | 31 Ari | | | | 31 Vir |

| JAN | FEB | MAR | APR | MAY | JUN | JUL | AUG | SEP | OCT | NOV | DEC |
|---|---|---|---|---|---|---|---|---|---|---|---|
| 2 Lib | 1 Sco | 2 Sag | 3 Aqu | 2 Pis | 3 Tau | 2 Gem | 1 Can | 2 Vir | 2 Lib | 1 Sco | 2 Cap |
| 4 Sco | 3 Sag | 4 Cap | 5 Pis | 4 Ari | 5 Gem | 5 Can | 3 Leo | 5 Lib | 4 Sco | 3 Sag | 4 Aqu |
| 6 Sag | 5 Cap | 6 Aqu | 7 Ari | 6 Tau | 7 Can | 7 Leo | 6 Vir | 7 Sco | 7 Sag | 5 Cap | 7 Pis |
| 8 Cap | 7 Aqu | 8 Pis | 9 Tau | 9 Gem | 10 Leo | 10 Vir | 8 Lib | 9 Sag | 9 Cap | 7 Aqu | 9 Ari |
| 10 Aqu | 9 Pis | 10 Ari | 11 Gem | 11 Can | 12 Vir | 12 Lib | 11 Sco | 12 Cap | 11 Aqu | 9 Pis | 11 Tau |
| 12 Pis | 11 Ari | 13 Tau | 14 Can | 14 Leo | 15 Lib | 15 Sco | 13 Sag | 14 Aqu | 13 Pis | 11 Ari | 13 Gem |
| 15 Ari | 13 Tau | 15 Gem | 16 Leo | 16 Vir | 17 Sco | 17 Sag | 15 Cap | 16 Pis | 15 Ari | 13 Tau | 15 Can |
| 17 Tau | 16 Gem | 17 Can | 19 Vir | 19 Lib | 19 Sag | 19 Cap | 17 Aqu | 18 Ari | 17 Tau | 16 Gem | 18 Leo |
| 19 Gem | 18 Can | 20 Leo | 21 Lib | 21 Sco | 21 Cap | 21 Aqu | 19 Pis | 20 Tau | 19 Gem | 18 Can | 20 Vir |
| 22 Can | 21 Leo | 22 Vir | 23 Sco | 23 Sag | 23 Aqu | 23 Pis | 21 Ari | 22 Gem | 22 Can | 21 Leo | 23 Lib |
| 24 Leo | 23 Vir | 25 Lib | 26 Sag | 25 Cap | 25 Pis | 25 Ari | 23 Tau | 24 Can | 24 Leo | 23 Vir | 25 Sco |
| 27 Vir | 25 Lib | 27 Sco | 28 Cap | 27 Aqu | 28 Ari | 27 Tau | 26 Gem | 27 Leo | 27 Vir | 26 Lib | 28 Sag |
| 29 Lib | 28 Sco | 29 Sag | 30 Aqu | 29 Pis | 30 Tau | 29 Gem | 28 Can | 29 Vir | 29 Lib | 28 Sco | 30 Cap |
| | | 31 Cap | | 31 Ari | | | 31 Leo | | | 30 Sag | |

| JAN | FEB | MAR | APR | MAY | JUN | JUL | AUG | SEP | OCT | NOV | DEC |
|---|---|---|---|---|---|---|---|---|---|---|---|
| 1 Aqu | 1 Ari | 1 Ari | 1 Gem | 1 Can | 2 Vir | 2 Lib | 1 Sco | 2 Cap | 1 Aqu | 2 Ari | 1 Tau |
| 3 Pis | 3 Tau | 3 Tau | 4 Can | 3 Leo | 5 Lib | 5 Sco | 3 Sag | 4 Aqu | 4 Pis | 4 Tau | 3 Gem |
| 5 Ari | 6 Gem | 5 Gem | 6 Leo | 6 Vir | 7 Sco | 7 Sag | 6 Cap | 6 Pis | 6 Ari | 6 Gem | 6 Can |
| 7 Tau | 8 Can | 7 Can | 9 Vir | 8 Lib | 10 Sag | 9 Cap | 8 Aqu | 8 Ari | 8 Tau | 8 Can | 8 Leo |
| 9 Gem | 10 Leo | 10 Leo | 11 Lib | 11 Sco | 12 Cap | 11 Aqu | 10 Pis | 10 Tau | 10 Gem | 10 Leo | 10 Vir |
| 12 Can | 13 Vir | 12 Vir | 14 Sco | 13 Sag | 14 Aqu | 13 Pis | 12 Ari | 12 Gem | 12 Can | 13 Vir | 13 Lib |
| 14 Leo | 16 Lib | 15 Lib | 16 Sag | 15 Cap | 16 Pis | 15 Ari | 14 Tau | 14 Can | 14 Leo | 15 Lib | 15 Sco |
| 17 Vir | 18 Sco | 17 Sco | 18 Cap | 18 Aqu | 18 Ari | 17 Tau | 16 Gem | 17 Leo | 17 Vir | 18 Sco | 18 Sag |
| 19 Lib | 20 Sag | 20 Sag | 20 Aqu | 20 Pis | 20 Tau | 20 Gem | 18 Can | 19 Vir | 19 Lib | 20 Sag | 20 Cap |
| 22 Sco | 23 Cap | 22 Cap | 22 Pis | 22 Ari | 22 Gem | 22 Can | 21 Leo | 22 Lib | 22 Sco | 23 Cap | 22 Aqu |
| 24 Sag | 25 Aqu | 24 Aqu | 24 Ari | 24 Tau | 25 Can | 24 Leo | 23 Vir | 24 Sco | 24 Sag | 25 Aqu | 24 Pis |
| 26 Cap | 27 Pis | 26 Pis | 27 Tau | 26 Gem | 27 Leo | 27 Vir | 26 Lib | 26 Sag | 26 Cap | 27 Pis | 27 Ari |
| 28 Aqu | | 28 Ari | 29 Gem | 28 Can | 29 Vir | 29 Lib | 28 Sco | 29 Cap | 29 Aqu | 29 Ari | 29 Tau |
| 30 Pis | | 30 Tau | 31 Leo | | | | 31 Sag | | 31 Pis | | 31 Gem |

# WHAT YOUR MOON SIGN SAYS ABOUT YOU

*Now that you know your Moon sign, read on to learn more about your emotional nature and your basic inner needs.*

## MOON IN ARIES

You have an emotional need to be first. And you want to be first *now* – there's no time to waste. Brimming with enthusiasm and energy, you love to keep busy and find waiting difficult. Remember to open up and talk to those closest to you about your feelings – they can help you to slow down and deal with any difficult emotions as they arise.

## MOON IN TAURUS

You love to be surrounded by beautiful possessions and enjoy food and clothes that make you feel good – you have a need for comfort. Familiarity and routine are important to you, and you don't deal well with sudden change. That stubborn streak means you're able to stand up for yourself and protect your own interests, just remember to relax once in a while and try new things.

## MOON IN GEMINI

Self-expression is one of your driving forces with this mix. Talking, drawing, writing – you simply have to communicate your feelings. And you love to listen to other peoples' ideas, too. To feed your curious intellect, you've probably got a tower of books and magazines at your bedside. Just don't forget to exercise your body as well as your mind.

## MOON IN CANCER

You were born to nurture others – whether that's through baking them a cake or being at the end of the phone when they need your reassuring words. Family is hugely important to you, and you want to feel loved and secure. Being honest about this and accepting your wonderfully sensitive and emotional nature will help you find inner peace.

## MOON IN LEO

You have an emotional need to be admired – all you really want is for everyone to love you. Your kind heart and generosity towards your friends and family means you are usually surrounded by others, and the attention you crave is easily won. When things don't go your way, you have a tendency to be dramatic – don't let your pride stop you from asking for help when you need it.

## MOON IN VIRGO

You are a gentle soul and appreciate the simple things in life. Helping others in small ways makes you feel needed, secure and purposeful. A clean and tidy environment is a must, and everything has to be in its proper place. Learning not to fuss when something isn't perfect is a challenge – look for useful ways to keep your practical nature busy and happiness will follow.

### MOON IN LIBRA

Close bonds are everything to you – you find strength and stability in your relationships with others. Your need for balance and harmony means you are an excellent peacemaker, skilled at helping people to see and understand another's perspective. Remember to feed your love of beauty with regular trips to art galleries and picturesque places.

### MOON IN SCORPIO

Deep and emotionally intense, you need to trust those close to you with your innermost thoughts and desires. All or nothing, you have incredible intuition and can see right to the heart of people. Finding one or two close friends who you can really open up to and be honest with about your feelings is important for your happiness. When this happens, your inner strength is unmatched.

### MOON IN SAGITTARIUS

Your need for freedom and space is overwhelming, but when you achieve it, you are bright, breezy and filled with a zest for life. Always on the lookout for new things to try and people to meet, your energy and enthusiasm lifts the spirits of those around you. Planning is not your strong suit; you prefer to go with the flow and see where it takes you – preferably somewhere fun and interesting!

### MOON IN CAPRICORN

Ambitious and practical, you want to work hard and achieve results. You are conscientious and naturally organized, with a clear picture of what you want and how you intend to get there. Remember to take time to kick back and relax – the strong front you present to those around you can hide your more sensitive side. Letting go occasionally isn't a sign of weakness.

### MOON IN AQUARIUS

Your desire to be unique and unusual is powerful, and you need the space and freedom to be yourself. Emotionally detached, you are happily independent and have an ability to see the bigger picture. Try not to lose touch with those closest to you – life is full of ups and downs, and friends and family can offer valuable support through tougher times.

### MOON IN PISCES

Dreamy and intuitive, your sensitive nature is highly attuned to the feelings of others. Be careful to steer clear of negative people – you're likely to absorb their vibes, and they will bring you down. It's important you learn how to take care of yourself when you feel overwhelmed emotionally. Escaping into a good book or listening to your favourite music can be a great way to re-set.

ELEMENTS

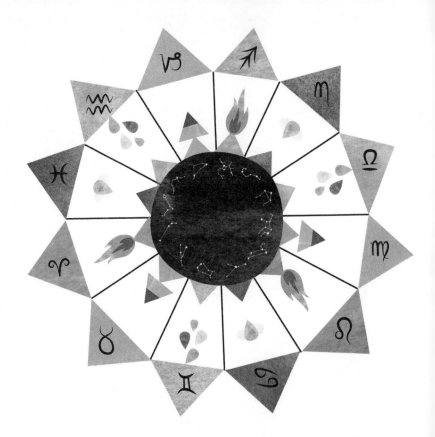

# YOUR ELEMENTAL TYPE

Fire, Earth, Air, Water – in ancient times these were thought to contain everything that existed on Earth. Today that's no longer the case, but there's no denying their powerful effect on people's lives. Think of the heat from the Sun, the way earth is used to grow food, the water you consume, the air that you breathe. And like so much in astrology, each element has two sides. You drink water and rain helps plants to grow, but the force of a tsunami can wreak havoc and destruction. You have all four elements within you, but one or more of them will stand out. You could be a single type, or a mix of two or three. Your elemental type says a lot about you and those you interact with. When you meet someone you feel naturally comfortable with, it's often because you are elementally compatible.

# IN YOUR ELEMENT

The most fixed of the Water signs, Scorpio could be compared to ice. Strong and silent on the outside (almost impenetrable), yet filled with mixed emotions. Capable and stoic, very few things faze you – you can handle things other people prefer not to talk about or face up to. At your best, you are tough and dependable, able to get to the emotional heart of things, to find the truth of the matter. At your worst you refuse to ask for support when it's needed and struggle alone.

 WATER WITH FIRE

Not an ideal mix. Water and Fire can be beautiful together, adventurous and dynamic, but if one is too dominant it can scorch Water's emotions or dampen Fire's energy. When it works, you will bring sensitivity and comfort, while Fire will provide motivation and the courage to act.

 WATER WITH EARTH

Comfortable and secure, you work wonderfully together, each helping the other to reach their potential. Earth is your rock, grounding you emotionally and helping you to get things done, while you refresh and enliven Earth.

 WATER WITH AIR

Air's detached, objective thinking can leave you thirsting for a deeper connection, but Air can also help Water to calm its emotional waves. However, just like a can of fizzy drink, all those bubbles can cause an explosion when shaken or put under pressure.

 WATER WITH WATER

Wonderfully compatible, your relationship is full of feeling, and you love just being together. Sometimes it can be difficult to tell where one ends and the other begins – hold onto your own identity and don't feel responsible for anyone else's feelings.

# THE MISSING PIECE

How dominant Water is within you depends on the influence of the other elements in your chart – ideally all four would be represented. Sometimes a lack of a particular element can cause an imbalance, making you feel rundown or stressed. The best way to counteract this is to tune in to the missing element and reharmonize yourself. Try the simple exercise below to get back in touch with any elements you're missing.

1. First, take a look at the Zodiac signs and their elements.

**Fire:** Aries, Leo, Sagittarius

**Earth:** Taurus, Virgo, Capricorn

**Air:** Gemini, Libra, Aquarius

**Water:** Cancer, Scorpio, Pisces

2. Now circle Water, as this is the element that represents your Sun sign. You're certain to have some of this element. Then do the same for your Moon sign and your Ascendant, circling the element associated with each.

3. Looking at the list, there should be one or more elements you haven't circled.

**Fire** – not enough Fire can leave you lacking in energy and motivation. You want to be more assertive and prepared to take the lead.

**Earth** – a lack of Earth can make you feel disorganized, off-balance or like you couldn't care less. You might want more routine, structure or to stay focused.

**Air** – Air will help you to communicate better, feel more sociable and lift your spirits. Use it to boost your curiosity and sharpen your wits.

4. Choose the element you would like to tune in to, whichever one you feel might benefit you the most. Then pick one of the ideas from the lists below. If Earth is missing, you could take a picnic to the park and sit on the grass. If it's Fire, you might turn your face to the sun and soak up its warmth. You can use this exercise whenever you feel out of balance.

### FIRE

Sunbathe
Toast marshmallows
Watch fireworks
Host a barbecue
Meditate on a candle flame
Catch the sunrise
Go stargazing

### EARTH

Grow tomatoes
Pick wildflowers
Camp in the garden
Do cartwheels on the grass
Build a sandcastle
Collect stones
Roll down a hill

### AIR

Fly a kite
Watch clouds go by
Blow bubbles
Feel the breeze
Play with a balloon
Chase butterflies
Breathe deep

We are
FAMILY

# WE'RE ALL IN THIS TOGETHER

When so much in your life is changing, your relationships with your parents can become even more important. If you're lucky, you get on well with yours, but even the most harmonious relationships can come under strain during the teenage years. How can astrology help? It can remind you that parents are people, too. They might not get everything right, but hopefully you believe that they have your best interests at heart. Learning more about who they are, why they do things and how you relate to them can make it easier for all of you to move forwards together.

## MOTHER MOON

The Moon sign you are born with can tell you a lot about how you see and treat your mother. This is because your Moon sign represents your emotional needs – what you need to feel safe and secure – and these are most often fulfilled by your mother. How you react to her can make a big difference to the way she behaves around you. If you are visibly upset by certain things she does, she is likely to change her behaviour the next time around. If you react with happiness and delight, she is more likely to repeat them.

*Here's how you see your mother according to your Moon sign . . .*

## ARIES

You view your mother as strong, honest and forthright. Sometimes, especially when she doesn't agree with your plans, this can make you feel as though she's taking over. Try not to push back too strongly, and remember she has your interests at heart.

## TAURUS

You like to feel your mother is looking after all of your everyday needs and is dependable and reliable. Don't judge her too harshly if she doesn't always live up to your expectations – providing for others is often a careful balancing act, and she is likely doing her best.

## GEMINI

Flighty and impulsive, you need your mother to give you the freedom to be yourself and make your own mistakes. Space and independence often have to be earned, though – what could you do to show her you're capable and trustworthy?

## CANCER

Your longing for your mother's emotional attention can give you a wonderful bond and connection. However, the slightest hint of rejection from her can wound you deeply. Try not to take her reactions personally – it's okay for her to make choices and have goals that differ from yours.

### LEO

You want to enjoy an open, honest relationship with your mother, where both of you say what you mean. Underlying this candour is a need for assurance and acceptance – when you feel vulnerable, be brave and explain to her how you feel.

### VIRGO

You are aware of who gives what in your emotional relationship with your mother, and occasionally this can make you feel that she isn't there for you. Viewing her actions as 'different' rather than 'wrong' will help you to trust she is doing what she thinks is right.

### LIBRA

You need your mother to recognize your emotional needs as valid and important. Try not to spend too much time putting others first – your relationship will flourish when you both accept the roles you play.

### SCORPIO

You want your mother to respect your emotional boundaries and allow you alone-time when you need it. The trust between you can be intense and unconditional, so much so you may have to remind her to step back occasionally.

## SAGITTARIUS

Upbeat and curious, your relationship works best when your mother is inspiring and encouraging, giving you the emotional freedom you need to expand your horizons. It's fine to chase independence, as long as you respect your mother's desire to give you roots.

## CAPRICORN

You empathize strongly with your mother's feelings, so when she's struggling, this can make you feel it's your fault. Learn to let go of this guilt – it's unintentional and unhelpful. Instead, recognize how much you need each other's emotional support and encouragement.

## AQUARIUS

You're not sure your mother's attempts to guide you are always necessary, and you don't like to burden her with your problems. Asking for help and talking things through might be more useful than you imagine and can bring you closer together at the same time.

## PISCES

Your mother's high expectations have made you stronger emotionally, even though there are times when you just want to feel like a child and let her take care of everything. Taking responsibility can be tough; don't be afraid to speak up when you need support.

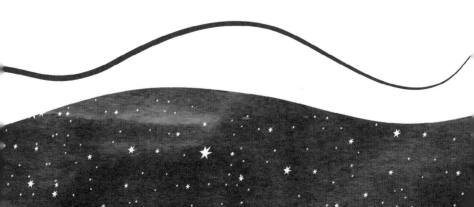

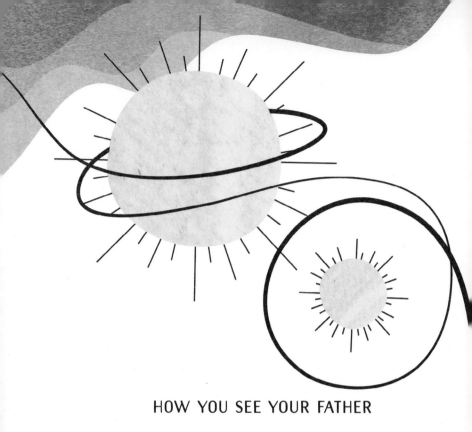

## HOW YOU SEE YOUR FATHER

Just as your Moon sign gives you an indication of how you see your mother, or whoever plays that nurturing role in your life, your Sun sign can reveal the way you view your father, or the caregiver who is most involved with discipline. Your relationship with this person is built over time. For girls, it can have a strong bearing on how you view any future romantic relationships, whereas boys will either rebel or identify with these traits.

You love your father, but wish he wasn't so clever at discovering your secrets. He just seems to *know*. Trust is a big deal to him, and you've worked hard to earn it. He is your greatest protector and if anyone upsets you, they'll be on the receiving end of that Scorpion sting.

Now read on to find out how your father's Sun sign affects your relationship . . .

*Your father's Sun sign will play a significant part in how you relate to him, and it can help you to understand why he acts the way he does – however infuriating it may sometimes seem!*

### ARIES

You love each other fiercely, but the struggle is real. It's irrelevant what you clash over: it's all about the winning between you two. In time you will develop a deep respect for each other and see the funny side of your animated relationship.

### TAURUS

There can be a blame-game in this relationship, with each one of you saying the other is too stubborn. Really, it's just that neither of you likes to back down. Learning how to reach a compromise will help harmony reign.

### GEMINI

Both of you are concerned with finding the truth of things. Your dad gets there through sheer intensity, while you figure it out rationally through experience and research. With luck, there's a meeting of minds and possibly even souls.

### CANCER

You both often try to hide your feelings underneath a tough outer shell. But if you can help to show your dad that it's okay to reveal vulnerability, you'll be more likely to enjoy your super-strong bond of trust and respect.

### LEO

Life can be a rollercoaster with you two in town. You are unapologetically dramatic, and your dad isn't always averse to the spotlight either. This just leaves the rest of your family to pull up their seats and watch the entertainment unfold.

### VIRGO

You are curious but in different ways. Your dad prefers to observe from the sidelines, whereas you rely on instinct and intuition. You could both benefit from lightening up – put your worries to one side occasionally and just enjoy the ride.

### LIBRA

You are united by the strong belief that everyone should follow their own path. Being true to yourself, however, can cause ripples in your relationship. If you try to work through any differences, it can help to strengthen the bond with your dad.

### SCORPIO

Scorpios are complicated. Your dad has had more time to get to grips with his complex nature and may be able to help you along. Generally, you dislike showing others if your feelings are hurt, but it's worth confiding in each other.

### SAGITTARIUS

There's a lovely learning curve in this relationship. While you share a sense of urgency about life, your father's encouragement often gives you the confidence to take more risks. This, in turn, can earn your loyalty.

### CAPRICORN

There's a basis for true understanding between you and your dad. While you might put on a different face to the outside world, when you are alone, it can seem easy. You could even end up going into business together.

### AQUARIUS

It's possible that you two will have your fair share of disputes because you are both headstrong. The good news, however, is that it's likely you'll end up admiring and even respecting each other, leading to a more settled relationship.

### PISCES

As a Scorpion, you find it difficult to trust, but your dad's faith in life can carry you along. This creates a playful dynamic as you both make exciting new discoveries about the world, and your relationship often gets better as you get older.

Best of
FRIENDS

# FRIENDS FOR LIFE

Friends play an essential role in your happiness. They can help you to move forwards when times are tough, see things from a new perspective and encourage you just to have fun. Every good friend you make has different qualities that will influence you and allow you to make more of your potential. A friend might show you it can be better to hold back when all you want to do is rush in, motivate you to stick with that project right to the end or inspire you to see an obstacle as a challenge. And astrology can be a great way to highlight those characteristics you're looking for in a friend. It can also tell you more about the type of friend you make for others.

## WHAT KIND OF FRIEND ARE YOU?

You're selective when it comes to making friends, but the friendships you do have are really special. Being highly perceptive, you choose your friends wisely, and your quiet self-confidence means you easily win them over. Once you've cemented a bond, you want to spend lots of time with your friends, welcoming them into your home and inner circle. You'll expect their loyalty in return, and if they betray you, you will seek revenge.

**Strengths:** *Passionate, hospitable, perceptive*
**Weaknesses:** *Guarded, jealous, suspicious*
**Friendship style:** *Intense, selective, highly loyal*

# IF YOUR BEST FRIEND IS . . .

### ARIES

Aries make friends easily. They're willing to help you achieve your goals, they see the best in you and they're happy to take risks for you, too. They love to be someone's best friend and can find it difficult to feel second to anyone else. They are always on the lookout for new, super-fun adventures and are happy to take you along for the ride. They have a knack for bringing people from all walks of life together.

**Strengths:** *Loyal, generous, fun-loving*
**Weaknesses:** *Insensitive, demanding, petulant*
**Friendship style:** *Busy, fun, warm*

### TAURUS

Considerate and charming, Taurus friends often have a talent for giving good advice. They like to take their time and allow friendships to develop slowly, but once you become close they treat you as a member of their family. As an Earth sign, they are dependable and grounded, and they make wonderful lifelong friends. Bear in mind they can place too much importance on material possessions, even judging others based on their wealth.

**Strengths:** *Caring, faithful, trustworthy*
**Weaknesses:** *Judgmental, stubborn, materialistic*
**Friendship style:** *Helpful, sweet, self-assured*

### GEMINI

You'll need lots of energy to keep up with a Gemini friend. They love to have fun, do crazy things and always have a story to tell. They'll make you laugh, but they can sometimes get a little carried away, perhaps exaggerating tales of their adventures in their effort to entertain you. They can be a bit gossipy, but they're not malicious. They're good listeners and will make you feel great, giving you lots of compliments – and always genuine ones, too.

**Strengths:** *Intelligent, energetic, fearless*
**Weaknesses:** *Impatient, easily bored, gossipy*
**Friendship style:** *Good listener, witty, spontaneous*

### CANCER

Once you form a close connection with Cancer, you have a friend who has your back. They're considerate and like nothing better than to make you feel happy. Watch out though; they're deeply emotional, which means that if you argue – even over something small – you'll have to work hard to patch things up again.

**Strengths:** *Loving, caring, intuitive*
**Weaknesses:** *Unforgiving, anxious, sensitive*
**Friendship style:** *Warm, affectionate, protective*

## LEO

As long as you don't expect too much from a Leo friend, you're in for a treat. Outgoing, confident and full of energy, they thrive on social occasions and love to be the life and soul of a party, making people laugh and being admired. They're good at bringing people together and are in high demand, so you won't always have them to yourself, but if you can tie them down you'll have some great quality one-on-one time.

**Strengths:** *Honest, brave, positive*
**Weaknesses:** *Arrogant, self-centred, proud*
**Friendship style:** *Supportive, cheerful, humorous*

## VIRGO

With a Virgo by your side you'll always have somewhere to go when times are tough. They'll be there for you, giving you well-thought-out advice and a gentle sympathetic ear. Even when there's not a crisis, they're charming and kind. They like to be organized, so if they make plans, make sure you stick to them. They won't let you down, but they'll expect the same from you in return.

**Strengths:** *Warm, modest, smart*
**Weaknesses:** *Shy, serious, overly critical*
**Friendship style:** *Fixer, good communicator, reliable*

## LIBRA

You can rely on your Libra friend to tell you how it is. They have a refreshing honesty, but they have a diplomatic way of sparing your feelings. They love spending time with you and like nothing better than a chat (especially if they're the one doing the talking!). They can always see both sides, so if there's a disagreement, it won't be for long.

**Strengths:** *Diplomatic, honest, sociable*
**Weaknesses:** *Indecisive, people pleaser, chatterbox*
**Friendship style:** *Laid-back, devoted, forgiving*

## SAGITTARIUS

Sagittarius are low-maintenance friends. Easy-going, positive and happy-go-lucky, they're up for anything. If you fancy an adventure, give them a call, but don't expect too much of them feelings-wise. Their friendship circle is wide and diverse, so you'll get to meet lots of interesting people, but they are easily bored and can struggle with emotional closeness. On the plus side, they won't put too many demands on you, so give them some space and enjoy the ride.

**Strengths:** *Adventurous, positive, open-minded*
**Weaknesses:** *Impatient, insensitive, easily bored*
**Friendship style:** *Generous, undemanding, never dull*

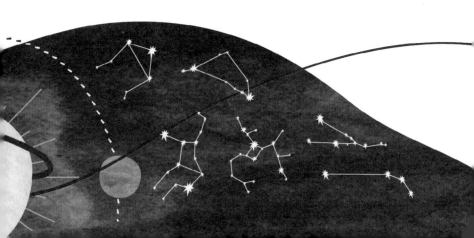

### CAPRICORN

You might have to put in some groundwork, but once you've cracked the seemingly aloof exterior of a Capricorn, you'll have yourself a genuine, warm, loving and faithful friend. They'll show you complete devotion, through the good times and the bad. They're thoughtful and sensible and will know when to call it a night, but they will often surprise you with their sly sense of humour. They love to make you smile.

**Strengths:** *Responsible, supportive, faithful*
**Weaknesses:** *Condescending, standoffish, serious*
**Friendship style:** *Thoughtful, rational, work hard/play hard*

### AQUARIUS

You'll have to share your Aquarius best friend – they'll probably flit in and out of lots of other friendships, too – but rest assured they've got your back and will go to the ends of the earth for you. They'll bring plenty of excitement and fun into your world, but they also treasure their alone-time, so don't put too many demands on them. They'll never pass judgment on you, no matter what you do.

**Strengths:** *Tolerant, independent, energetic*
**Weaknesses:** *Easily bored, rebellious, forgetful*
**Friendship style:** *Fun, exciting, unpredictable*

### PISCES

A Pisces friend is a great listener who is sympathetic and caring and will always make time for you. They're the perfect friend if you need a shoulder to cry on, but they can sometimes get too emotionally involved. If there is any discord in your friendship, they are quick to blame themselves. Reassure them and let them know it's not their fault and you'll soon win back their love and support.

**Strengths:** *Loving, caring, good listener*
**Weaknesses:** *Sensitive, self-pitying, insecure*
**Friendship style:** *Supportive, sympathetic, selfless*

# Your BIRTHDAY log

*List the birthdays of your family and friends and discover their Sun signs*

# ARIES

March 21–April 20

*Passionate, energetic, impulsive*

# TAURUS

April 21–May 21

*Steady, tenacious, trustworthy*

# GEMINI

May 22–June 21

*Intelligent, outgoing, witty*

# CANCER

## June 22–July 22

*Caring, home-loving, affectionate*

# LEO

July 23–August 23

*Loud, big-hearted, fun*

# VIRGO

*Organized, modest, responsible*

......................................................................................

......................................................................................

......................................................................................

......................................................................................

......................................................................................

......................................................................................

......................................................................................

......................................................................................

......................................................................................

......................................................................................

......................................................................................

......................................................................................

......................................................................................

......................................................................................

......................................................................................

......................................................................................

......................................................................................

......................................................................................

......................................................................................

......................................................................................

......................................................................................

......................................................................................

......................................................................................

# LIBRA

September 23–October 22

*Charming, creative, graceful*

# SCORPIO

October 23–November 21

*Powerful, mysterious, magnetic*

# SAGITTARIUS

November 22–December 21

*Adventurous, optimistic, lucky*

# CAPRICORN

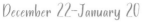

December 22–January 20

*Ambitious, dedicated, serious*

# AQUARIUS

January 21–February 19

*Eccentric, independent, imaginative*

# PISCES

*Dreamy, sensitive, compassionate*

Lucky in
LOVE

# WHY OPPOSITES REALLY DO ATTRACT

The sign opposite your Ascendant (your Rising sign) on your birth chart reveals who you will attract, and who will attract you. Known as your Descendant, it's the constellation that was setting on the Western horizon at the moment and place you were born.

This sign is everything you are not – a kind of mirror image, or two sides of the same coin.

Yet, strangely, you are often drawn to the qualities of this sign over and over again in the people you meet. It's possible that these characteristics are ones you feel you lack yourself, and you sense that the other person can fill in what's missing. Sometimes it really is true that opposites attract!

| Ascendant | Descendant |
|-----------|------------|
| Aries | Libra |
| Taurus | Scorpio |
| Gemini | Sagittarius |
| Cancer | Capricorn |
| Leo | Aquarius |
| Virgo | Pisces |
| Libra | Aries |
| Scorpio | Taurus |
| Sagittarius | Gemini |
| Capricorn | Cancer |
| Aquarius | Leo |
| Pisces | Virgo |

# WHAT DO YOU LOOK FOR?

*Once you've matched up your Ascendant with your Descendant from the list on the previous page, you can get to know the qualities that are most likely to attract you. You can use this information whether you're thinking about romance or friendship.*

### LIBRA DESCENDANT

You're looking for balance and harmony in your relationship, with someone who makes you feel interesting and important. You want to be listened to and value the ability to compromise. Gentleness and sensitivity are the qualities you're searching for.

### SCORPIO DESCENDANT

You want an intense, passionate relationship with someone who will welcome you wholeheartedly into their world and want to spend lots of time with you. You are attracted to someone who will take control, but who will also look out for you and protect you.

### SAGITTARIUS DESCENDANT

Adventure and fun are what you crave when it comes to love. You want someone open-minded who will accept you for who you are. You need to be given plenty of space to breathe and not be stifled by too many demands.

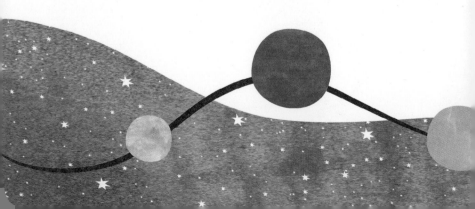

## CAPRICORN DESCENDANT

You seek total dedication and devotion from those you love. You're happy to take your time and let a relationship develop naturally, and aren't put off by someone who appears cool or guarded. You like a cheeky sense of humour, too.

## AQUARIUS DESCENDANT

You are attracted to someone who is independent and has a full life outside of your relationship, although you want to know that if push comes to shove, they will be right there for you. You like to be kept on your toes.

## PISCES DESCENDANT

You're not afraid of a deep relationship with someone who wears their heart on their sleeve. You want to be cared for, emotionally supported and loved unconditionally. You want to be the centre of someone's world.

### ARIES DESCENDANT

You like someone to spar with and who lets you have your own way, but is still strong enough to put their foot down when the gravity of the situation demands it. You will need to respect your partner's strength, bravery and integrity.

### TAURUS DESCENDANT

Stability and reliability are high on your list of priorities when it comes to forming relationships. You dislike chaos and are drawn to people who you know won't surprise or disappoint you. Instead you want a partnership that's grounded and safe.

### GEMINI DESCENDANT

You're attracted to someone who is spontaneous and fearless, and who can keep you entertained. You're likely to fall for someone who makes you feel super-special and is quick to recognize your achievements and boost your confidence.

### CANCER DESCENDANT

You seek relationships where you're made to feel like one of the family, where your every need and demand is met, particularly emotionally. You want to feel warm and fuzzy and protected by those you love.

### LEO DESCENDANT

You're drawn to someone who is strong, confident and outgoing with a busy social life but who can also give you warmth and passion when required. You're attracted to those who can make you laugh and sweep you off your feet.

### VIRGO DESCENDANT

You long for kindness and tenderness in a partnership, along with reliability. You want someone who can bring order into your life and who will think things through in a methodical way. Nothing should be left to chance.

Life at
SCHOOL

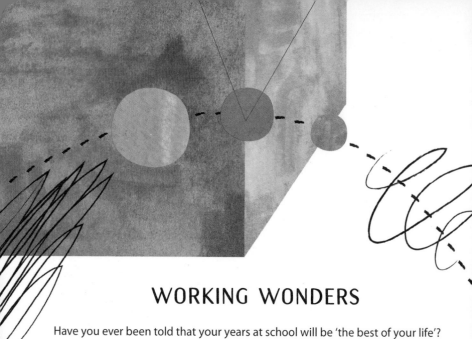

# WORKING WONDERS

Have you ever been told that your years at school will be 'the best of your life'? Do you think they will be? Why? Many different things will determine how much you enjoy your school days. And there are sure to be ups and downs along the way. But there are a couple of important factors that astrology can help with. The first is determining your skills and strengths, and the second is learning to work well with others. Identifying your natural interests and abilities can help you to develop a sense of purpose, and it's this that is most likely to motivate you to work hard and actually have fun while you do it. To have a sense of purpose, you need to know yourself and what it is you want from your life. Not what others want for you, or what is expected of you, but what actually makes you come alive.

## HIDDEN TALENTS

Not all of your attributes will be immediately obvious. Just because you're a Scorpio doesn't mean you are always secretive, for example. You can think about what a typical Scorpio might be good at, but you are unique, and the stars are only a guide. Think about your strengths – both emotional and physical. The examples on the right may strike a chord with you, or you might want to create your own list.

## BECAUSE YOU'RE ... CAUTIOUS

You are a careful thinker and prefer one-to-one communication to large groups.
You don't like to take risks, have good judgment, and a talent for solving problems.

*Maybe you could be a ...*
chemist, detective, pharmacist

## BECAUSE YOU'RE ... ANALYTICAL

You use facts and logic when making decisions. Ruled by the head
rather than the heart, you are not easily swayed in emotional arguments.
You are excellent with data.

*Maybe you could be a ...*
scientist, auditor, researcher

## BECAUSE YOU'RE ... CARING

You like to work with other people, especially when their wellbeing
and development is the focus of your work

*Maybe you could be a ...*
psychiatrist, therapist, hypnotist

## BECAUSE YOU'RE . . . A LEADER

You love to persuade other people to do something, buy something or believe in your cause. You're great at influencing and motivating others.

*Maybe you could be a . . .*
business developer, entrepreneur

## BECAUSE YOU'RE . . . DETERMINED

You enjoy completing tasks and persevere to finish what you started. You work hard to reach your goals and keep going even when things aren't working out.

*Maybe you could be a . . .*
surgeon, human resources manager

# FAMOUS SCORPIO PEOPLE

Pablo Picasso – *Artist*
Marie Antoinette – *The last Queen of France*
Katy Perry – *Pop singer*
Marie Curie – *Physicist and chemist*
Bill Gates – *Founder of Microsoft*
Drake – *Entrepreneur and recording artist*
Leonardo DiCaprio – *Actor*
Emma Stone – *Actor*

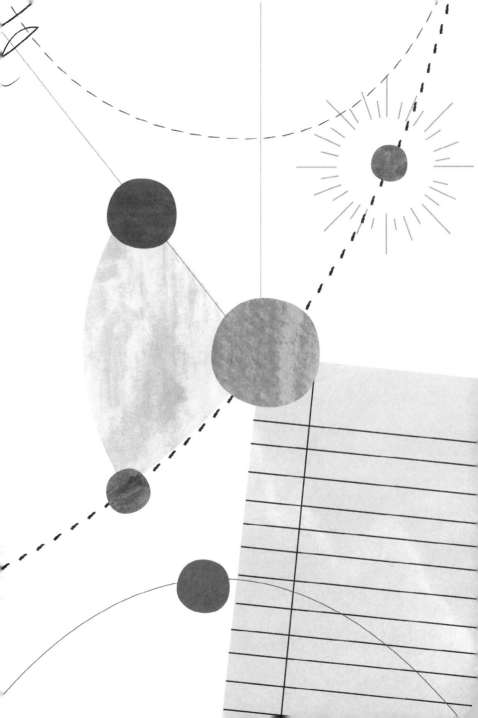

# TEAM WORK

*Working together with others is essential for almost any career path you choose to follow in later life. School can be competitive, yet working in collaboration with your peers rather than against them builds skills that today's employers are looking for.*

*Here's how well you work together with . . .*

## ARIES

Underneath that cool and calm exterior, you're as ambitious and determined as Aries. You're just not as vocal about it. You admire and respect their honesty and passion and will watch their back, especially if you're working in a competitive environment.

## TAURUS

You're both prone to stubbornness, but as long as you learn to back down occasionally, this could be a fruitful union. You're opposite signs of the Zodiac, so things could get complicated at times, but your individual strengths and weaknesses balance each other out and can create something truly memorable.

## GEMINI

On paper this might not look like the best of pairings, but give this one a chance. Let Gemini come up with the ideas while you back them up with in-depth research. You won't be afraid to say if the ideas don't stack up either. At least they'll know where they stand.

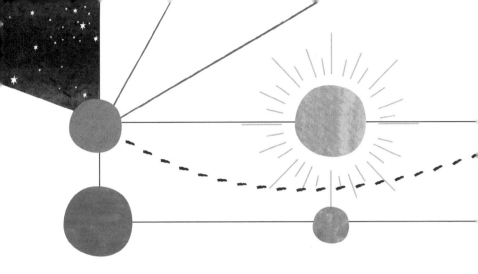

### CANCER

Both Water signs, neither of you will be satisfied with just getting the job done. You'll both want to go deeper than that, analysing problems and finding solutions. As a pair, you're a great asset to any team, but don't be resentful if others don't put in the same level of effort.

### LEO

This can be a battle of wills at times, with both sides craving attention and recognition, but if you want to succeed you'll have to put your egos to one side. Ultimately you both want the same thing – to be the very best – so settle your disagreements and focus on the wider objective. It'll be easier that way.

### VIRGO

As long as you give it time to develop, wonderful things can come out of a Scorpio–Virgo partnership. You might need to tread carefully at first, but you will eventually earn Virgo's trust and bring out the best in your teammate. Embrace each other's differences, and you could be a powerful pair.

### LIBRA

You're both committed to the job, but communication might be an issue between you two. While Libra is a natural communicator, it's not your strong point, and this might stifle any constructive teamwork. If things get too bad, try conversing online, or you could always bring in a mediator?

### SCORPIO

It's not always easy to work with someone so like yourself, especially for emotional and distrusting Scorpio. But if you can get on the same page and channel your shared determination and resourcefulness, you can accomplish great things. Trust each other.

### SAGITTARIUS

You might have completely different ideas about how to get there, but at least you both agree that you want to succeed. To get the best out of this partnership, Scorpio needs to open up a bit – it will pay off in the end – and Sagittarius might do well to think before they speak.

### CAPRICORN

Strong ambition on both sides will ensure this team will flourish. You'll come up with the strategic ideas, and Capricorn will give them structure. You'll work well on setting up a new business or venture and will probably end up being lifelong friends.

### AQUARIUS

You're both often misunderstood by those around you, but that doesn't mean you understand each other any better. The trouble is, you're both convinced you're right and find it hard to listen. You both have a lot to offer, but one of you will need to back down, just once in a while.

### PISCES

You're both dedicated and passionate workers but don't always get the credit you deserve. Neither of you are good at shouting about your work, so your team achievements can get overlooked. Next time, don't be afraid to show off a bit. It's time for your successes to be recognized.

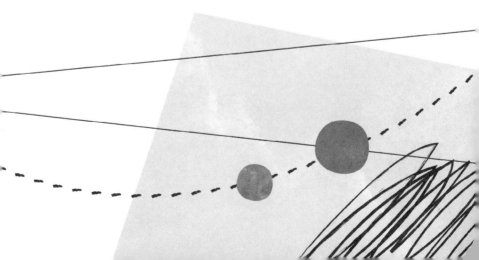

First published 2019
by Ammonite Press
an imprint of Guild of Master Craftsman Publications Ltd
Castle Place, 166 High Street, Lewes, East Sussex, BN7 1XU
United Kingdom

www.ammonitepress.com

Copyright in the Work © GMC Publications Ltd, 2019

Editorial: Susie Duff, Jane Roe, Rachel Roberts, Paul Wade
Designer: Jo Chapman
Illustrations: Sara Thielker
Cover illustration: Sara Thielker

ISBN 978-1-78145-401-5

Colour reproduction by GMC Reprographics
Printed and bound in China

AMMONITE
PRESS